THE SHORT AND BLOODY HISTORY OF SPIES

THE SHORT AND BLOODY HISTORY OF SPIES

John Farman

⌐ Lerner Publications Company/Minneapolis

First American edition published in 2002 by Lerner Publications Company

Copyright © 2000 by John Farman

This book is available in two editions:
Library binding by Lerner Publications Company, a division of Lerner Publishing Group
Soft cover by First Avenue Editions, an imprint of Lerner Publishing Group
241 First Avenue North
Minneapolis, MN 55401 U.S.A.

Website address: www.lernerbooks.com

Library of Congress Cataloging-in-Publication Data

Farman, John.
   The short and bloody history of spies / by John Farman—1st
American ed.
      p.   cm.
   Includes index.
   Summary: A humorous presentation of the history of espionage
and the stories of individual spies from around the world.
   ISBN: 0-8225-0845-1 (lib. bdg. : alk. paper)
   ISBN: 0-8225-0846-X (pbk. : alk. paper)
   1. Espionage—History—Juvenile literature. 2. Spies—Juvenile
literature. [1. Espionage—History. 2. Spies.] I. Title.
UB270.5 .F37 2002
327.12'09—dc21   2001050688

Manufactured in the United States of America
1 2 3 4 5 6 – JR – 07 06 05 04 03 02

CONTENTS

PSST! WANNA KNOW ALL ABOUT SPIES?

Most people think of spies as dark, shadowy men with big brimmed hats, fake mustaches, and no friends. Most of the time they aren't (and weren't) anything like that. There have always been almost as many women as men in the spying game, and nine times out of ten you wouldn't have known if you met one. Just like zebras wear stripes so as not to stand out in the environment where they live, and chameleons change color for just about the same reason, spies are most notable for not being notable. Let's face it, your teacher, your dentist, that funny guy who works in the library, or even your own mom or dad could be one—and you would never know anything about it. Spooky or what?

So What and Who Is a Spy?

Spies are those guys who are paid to move quietly among a group of people to find out secret stuff that another group (the ones who pay them) want to hear about. Spies are thus sort of professional tattletales. So why would anyone want to pass on the secrets of those who appear to be their friends to people who appear not to be? Surely that's a really mean thing to do. Oddly enough, a spy can usually get away with anything—lying, cheating, stealing, even murdering, and still not be thought badly of—it's all part of the game called espionage.

Most of the time, spies spy for political reasons—because they don't like how another country runs its business. This was very much the case during what was called the Cold War between the Soviet Union's Communist government and the democratic government of the United States. This war started in 1945 as soon as the Allies beat the Germans in World War II. To be fair, these spies were almost the most forgivable ones, for at least they believed that what they were doing was for the good of humankind. Whether they were right or wrong is not for me to say. Either way, practically every country in the world spies on every other country in the world—it's a fact.

Example

Despite the Soviet Union's rather unexpected fall in 1991, resulting in the dismantling of the infamous KGB (its spy agency), Russia now boasts four intelligence services and keeps squillions of spies in embassies throughout the world. Other sorts of spies, of course, don't do it for nice, moral reasons, and they never care about high-flown ideologies like Communism or capitalism. They're the ones who work purely for the money. This sort of behavior is becoming more and more the case in big business, where huge amounts of money change hands for details about a rival's strategies or products. The recipe for Coca-Cola, for instance, is famous for being one of the most guarded and sought-after secrets ever, and rivals would pay a king's ransom for the hidden ingredient.

But . . .

. . . that's just the simple side of things. Have you ever heard of counterespionage or of such a thing as a double agent? This is where it all gets tricky. Counterspies or double agents are the ones that one side thinks are working for them but who really turn out to be working for the people whom they are supposed to be spying on—or sometimes even both . . . a classic double bluff. They often give their clients (the ones buying the secrets) a whole bunch of false information, simply to lead them away from the real plot. The best thing about this scenario is that the spy in question usually gets paid by both sides, a sort of double whammy. The worst thing about this

scenario is that when the people who first employed them, or even the second people who employed them, find out they've been double-crossed, they get very annoyed. That's generally how more than a few spies end up wearing stylish concrete boots and being shoved over tall bridges into deep water and seldom heard of again.

Mole Hunt!

Very often a spy will stay in the same job for years while leaking little tidbits of information every now and again to the enemy or business rivals. Not from the likes of hairdressers or gardeners, I must add, but companies where either the inside information is useful to another country (weapons etc.) or to a business competitor (car manufacturers etc.). These people are called "moles," presumably because they operate "underground" and for the most part invisibly.

Good Tools

As technology develops, so do the tools that a country or company can use to spy. Real life constantly leaves James Bond with his 007 pants down. There are pin-sized microphones that operate on their own (without wires), tiny little cameras that work in the dark, and computers that can hack into others even though there seems to be no connection. These gadgets are all commonplace. So much so, that really important meetings, political or otherwise, have to be held in unbuggable, hard-to-reach places.

Old News

But trying to find out other people's secrets is nothing new. Nosy individuals have been trying to get away with such behavior almost since the beginning of time. This little book will attempt to trace espionage from its very beginnings, tell you who were the best and worst people at it, and give you a little bit of the day-to-day life of a spy.

EARLY DAYS

Spying is one of the oldest professions. The problem with spying is that it tends to be done in secret, so a lot of the really successful spying operations went on without anyone managing to write much about them—good for the spies but bad for history. Obviously, this becomes problematic when writing a book about the subject, but there seem to be a few names that crop up every time I dive into the deep and dusty records.

Sun-tzu

Just like everything else, spying seems to have begun in China. Try as I might, I can't find any records of espionage that go back beyond 510 B.C., when a Chinese man called Sun-tzu, wrote a book called *Ping Fa* or, if your Chinese isn't up to par, *The Art of War*.

It was all about how to get yourself a real secret service with spies and stuff and how to use them when having a war—which seemed to occur all the time in ancient China. This book was so good that it became compulsory reading for Chinese generals and military men. In fact, the tactics of the World War II Japanese attack on Pearl Harbor in 1941 came straight from the pages of *Ping Fa*. When American scholars realized this, they decided it might be smart to get it translated into English as well.

One of the most famous lines in the book went something like: "Those who know the enemy as well as themselves will never suffer defeat." Also: "Foreknowledge enables sovereigns and commanders to strike and conquer and achieve things beyond the reach of ordinary men."

Pay attention to this next story because I'm going to test you on it later.

Sun-tzu came from Ch'i but lived in Wu. King Ho Lu read *Ping Fa* and made Sun-tzu head of his troops. Sun-tzu defeated Ch'u and entered the capital Ying before turning his attention to Ch'i and Ching. Clear? Good.

Sun-tzu described every type of spy and claimed that they must be honored above everybody else in the land. He liked the idea of seeking out enemy spies and being so nice to them (free takeout, etc.) that they'd come over to his side and spy on their old bosses while telling them lies about his troops.

Test

Without looking:

Who was Ho Lu?

Who read *Ping Fa?*

What was the capital of Ch'u?

Who came from Wu?

And, most of all . . . Wu cares?

Alexander the Great

The next person I turned up was Alexander the Great, of all people. Alexander, who lived in the fourth century B.C., was the son of the mighty Philip II of Macedon and had been taught everything he knew by the philosopher Aristotle. Alex loved the idea of passing secret messages and snooping on his own troops to see who was or wasn't plotting. His sneaky methods must have worked, because he used them to find out who had killed his dad. Later, these ideas helped when he decided to go a-conquering (as they all did). Starting out in 334 B.C., his armies managed to crush lots of different peoples—the Triballi, the Getae, the Illyrians, the Thebans, the Persians, the Lycians, the Pisidians, the Egyptians, the Tyrians, the Ouxians, the Mardi, the Scythians, the Massagetai, not to mention all the Indians (in India). And, after lunch, the . . .

A Clever Espionage Trick

Alexander was fond of sending identical scrolls wrapped around staffs. He hid the secret message within a fairly ordinary boring report. The parchment was wound around and around a staff in a spiral, and the message was written along it in line with the staff. Unwound it made no sense whatsoever. Wrapped around a staff of identical width it could be read again. Get it? This idea survived right into the twentieth century and became the blueprint for many codes. A thin strip of paper can be wrapped tightly around a pencil and the message written along the line of the pencil. When the paper's pulled out it reads as pure nonsense. Try it.

14

The Roman Republic

The Romans didn't create a massive empire without a large amount of undercover work. Many Roman authors of the time let it be known that espionage was widespread and that the Romans had a huge network of spies resident in foreign lands. They also had double agents (called *exploratores*) who posed as friends of Rome's enemies while all the time sending back lots of juicy stuff about their armies, like where they went and when. At home, they took the form of a sort of underground police (kind of like the Gestapo in World War II Germany), infiltrating any groups who looked as though they might be planning to attack their emperor or his men.

The *speculatores* were another bunch attached to each Roman legion as secret service operators. They even had a club called the *schola speculatorum,* where they'd meet and swap tall stories and tricky trade secrets.

Henry II

In the higher circles of espionage, a term exists and is used as a warning to all would-be renegades even to this day. It's called "the Henry II syndrome." It all started in the 1100s, with the serious rift between King Henry II of England and his archbishop of Canterbury, Thomas à Becket. The archbishop was becoming annoyingly fond of the doings of the Roman Catholics and the pope. Unfortunately, his old friend Henry most certainly wasn't. It was when the archbishop started excommunicating (throwing out of the church) lots of Henry's favorite servants that the king began to really get upset. One day Henry happened to say, almost in passing, to four of his most favored knights, "Who will rid me of this turbulent priest?" The knights, who were extremely anxious to please, took him at his word. That night they went to Canterbury (where the archbishops of Canterbury usually live) and promptly went at him with their freshly sharpened swords. Unfortunately, Henry hadn't meant that at all and suffered terrible guilt for causing the death of someone who had once been his best friend.

In modern spying circles, therefore, they use the term "Henry II syndrome" as a warning to anyone who takes a politician's or a military leader's idle comment seriously (perish the thought), or who simply carries out an action on their own to gain favor.

By the Way
It all turned out all right for Thomas in the end (apart from being murdered) as he was made a saint in 1173.

Blondel

King Richard the Lion-Hearted (the one Robin Hood made all the fuss about) was best friends with a French guy called Blondel de Nesle. Blondel accompanied Richard on his campaign in the Holy Land to thwart the mighty Saladin (head of the Muslim army). In 1192 Richard rushed through Austria on his way home to rein in his crafty brother John. But en route poor Richard was captured and held for ransom in a secret castle by the duke of Austria (they did a lot of that sort of thing in those days).

Back home, it seemed fairly natural and appropriate for the king's loyal followers to ask Blondel to go on a spying mission to find his boss—but he'd have to have a disguise. We next hear of Monsieur de Nesle in heavy disguise, dressed as a silly-looking traveling minstrel (bells on pointy hat and stuff), trudging his way through Germany and into Austria. Blondel paused outside every castle to sing Richard's favorite tune (favorite because Richard composed it). He also presumably had to pretend to be German. Blondel was singing away outside some old Austrian castle when he heard the faint voice of his old friend joining in with the chorus. The spying had paid off. Blondel dashed home to England, raised the

SOUNDS FAMILIAR

17

ransom that the greedy Austrian duke had demanded, and got his best friend, the king, out.

I'd like to report that they lived happily ever after, but a little later Richard died while trying to get back the part of France that he'd once owned. He was only forty-one. Rotten luck, really. He was hit by a bolt from the very weapon (the crossbow) that he'd introduced to France! *Quel dommage!!*

The Ninjas

Would you believe it? Those ludicrous half-men/half-turtles called the Ninja Turtles really existed (well, just the ninja part) way back in twelfth-century Japan. They were a subbranch of the famous samurai who were probably the bravest warriors that ever lived. Back in those days, big rifts existed between all the ruling families in Japan. But by 1189, a man called Yoritomo became supreme shogun—the Japanese name for a military leader. He was the first to train ninjas to go on special spying missions to find out what his enemies were up to. These very fit young men trained from the age of five. They learned to hang from branches for ages (for some little-remembered reason), swim underwater for long distances, walk tightropes (for spying on circuses), and make and operate machines to help them fly. Best of all, they learned *ninjitsu*— the ancient art of disguises and tricks to make themselves invisible.

CAN YOU SEE ME NOW?

Genghis Khan

The mighty Genghis Khan was born under the name Temüjin in 1167 by Lake Baikal, in Russia. His dad ruled the land between the Amur River and the Great Wall of China (built to keep him and all his Mongolkind out).

Temüjin took over when only thirteen and struggled to keep his position, as the rest of his tribe were always revolting (in every way possible). A legendary leader, a skilled horseman, and a fierce fighter, he soon had his tribe and the neighboring tribes under control. By 1206 these barbarians decided to make him their leader, calling him Genghis ("precious warrior" in Chinese) and Khan ("lord" in Turkish). Flushed with success, Genghis Khan began to look for new pastures to conquer, for the Mongols needed more grass on which to feed their millions of horses.

He began to wonder what exactly was over that Great Wall. So in 1213 he and his horrible hordes invaded China (and presumably ate all their grass). The rest is history and not for this little book, but it must be said that Genghis Khan became known as the greatest military leader the world has ever seen.

19

His success not only lay in his merciless savagery but in his use of intelligence to figure out the weaknesses of his enemies. One of his best tricks was to send his most trusty scouts to his foes. The scouts claimed to be deserters and that they really didn't want to be Mongols anymore. When these spies found out all they needed to know, they snuck back to the Mongols and spilled the beans.

Also Genghis asked his traveling merchants and traders to double as spies in order to update him on what went on in foreign lands. A unique early mail service quickly relayed information to the lord and master despite massive distances. This involved a rider in a special kind of Mongol mailman's outfit, dashing at full speed (upon a horse, of course) between staging points that sat twelve fast-galloping hours apart and had fresh horses waiting. It was said that a single rider could achieve three hundred miles in a day (not to mention a very sore backside).

By the Way

This system apparently gave the idea, centuries later, to the men who set up the Pony Express in the Wild West.

Council of Ten (Fourteenth Century)

In Venice during the Renaissance period in the 1300s, the Doge (chief magistrate), Marino Faliero, headed a conspiracy designed to topple the sovereignty of the noblemen of the Venetian Republic. Faliero was found out and executed in 1355 for his trouble.

To counteract this sort of unsociable behavior, a group called the Consiglio degli Dieci (Council of Ten) was set up. This spooky bunch acted as official snoopers or spies. They controlled the secret police, were involved in espionage and counterespionage, and had almost unlimited power. They wore sinister masks at official gatherings so as not to be recognized but would open their long cloaks, if challenged, to flash the official insignia that was woven into their linings.

By the Way

Venetian counterintelligence agents successfully outwitted industrial spies from Genoa, another Italian city. The Venetians' sworn enemies were trying to steal their secret methods of making their internationally admired cannons.

Sir Francis Walsingham

If ever there was a time when England needed a real live secret service, it was in the 1500s during the reign of Queen Elizabeth I. Sir Francis Walsingham was her undersecretary and soon realized that far too many foreign, particularly French, characters hung around the dark alleys of London— probably up to no good. France, by the way, was England's very worst enemy and had a well-developed spy network. Walsingham got the Lord Mayor to keep a weekly list of all foreigners arriving and leaving the city and had routine checks to see what they were up to.

Walsingham became the ambassador to France in 1570, in an effort to cool things down between the two countries. Actually, if truth be told, it gave him a better chance to set up a network of spies in France. Poor Francis, by the way, had to finance all these shady characters out of his own pocket—as the meanie old queenie was infamous for keeping the royal pursestrings tightly knotted. "Knowledge is never too dear (costly)," Walsingham pleaded in vain.

He eventually came home in 1573 to become the queen's first secretary and a member of the Privy Council. Everyone knew that his real job was still to keep a watchful eye abroad using all the new contacts he'd made.

It was still costing him a fortune. Francis eventually went belly-up financially due to almost single-handedly financing England's intelligence service overseas. It was a shame really, for at the time all those fearful foreigners were spending far more on theirs.

This underfinancing was dangerous in other ways. When European diplomats realized how little the poor English diplomats were actually paid, they dangled bags of gold in front of them in order to gain their services. This

strategy worked on several occasions. Sir Edward Stafford, for one, went over as ambassador to France, but the Spaniards (who were planning to invade England) soon noticed how "broke" he was. He became their agent. Although found out eventually, he was never brought to trial. Dear old Eddie must have worked as a double agent, certainly giving the Spaniards trivial information but all the time keeping Walsingham up to date on them. Nice one!

Walsingham battled on, and by 1587 he convinced his colleagues (and the queen) that the biggest threat came from Spain (England's new worst enemy). He decided this because one of his top men (Richard Gibbes) kept warning him every five minutes of a massive armada (fleet) of 150 ships that had gathered in Spain and were, to put it mildly, all pointing toward England! As cover, Gibbes had posed as a supporter of the Catholic Mary Queen of Scots who the Spaniards wanted on England's throne.

Walsingham stepped up his secret service to such a point that he no longer just listened to what was going on in deepest Spain. Better than all that, he had people right in the thick of the Spanish court and even managed to influence the date for their long-awaited attack on England. By twisting the arms of King Philip's bankers in Genoa, he held up the loans Spain needed for putting the finishing touches on their fleet (guns, sails, flags, and things). The fleet sailed but was soundly defeated by the English.

There is no doubt that one of the reasons the Spanish lost was because England's little fleet knew all about them. Better still, thanks to Richard Gibbes, the English knew exactly at what time they'd turn up (2:15 on Tuesday). Thanks to espionage, England didn't become part of the Spanish empire.

Gilbert Gifford

Gifford was a young Catholic languishing in jail on a charge of fraud during the reign of Elizabeth I. When he was released, he went to work for Mary Queen of Scots (the one who Liz thought was trying to overthrow her) but offered himself to Walsingham as a spy in her camp. He read all her secret messages, which were left in barrels and wine bottles. Best of all, he was let in on the elusive code that the pope used for all his letters and stuff. This meant that Walsingham, and therefore Queen Elizabeth, could second guess just about every move the enemy made. Eventually, they were able to uncover the final plot against Liz, which led to the severe removal of cousin Mary's still pretty head on February 8, 1587.

Christopher Marlowe

Many people believe that the playwright Christopher Marlowe wrote quite a few of the plays that Will Shakespeare got the credit for. He was certainly around at the same time and was certainly very good at it (playwriting).

Marlowe was the second son of a Cambridge shoemaker and went to Cambridge University in 1579. He nearly didn't get his degree because, toward the end of his studies, he was hardly ever there (I know the feeling). Luckily, a letter turned up from the Privy Council in the nick of time saying that he'd been in London "on matters touching the benefit of his country."

Chris, as it turned out, was in Queen Elizabeth's secret service. Sir Francis Walsingham had been employing a few of the brighter Cambridge undergraduates (always good for recruitment spies) and sending them over to Rheims in France. Rheims was a hotbed for spies and counterspies. Pretending to be a Catholic, he got in with the duke of Guise, the king of Spain's friend, and had a great time finding out the names of Catholic conspirators stationed in England.

It all went downhill however, as that sort of thing so often did (and does). The next we hear of our Chris was in 1593, when he was arrested for reasons unknown. He was released on bail, but ten days later the playwright was dead, killed in a bar brawl. His killer, surprisingly, was given a free pardon, so it really isn't hard to figure out that poor Chris was probably intentionally murdered. Why? I bet Queen Elizabeth might have been able to tell you.

Oliver Cromwell

Have you ever wondered how Oliver Cromwell, head of the army on the side of the rebel Roundheads, managed to defeat King Charles I in the English civil war of 1640? Probably not. Well, I'll tell you anyway. It was largely because of his deep belief in the merits of spying. Despite the Royalists' best efforts to keep their mouths shut, the rebel Roundheads seemed to end up with secrets galore, almost solely through Cromwell's head of intelligence, a real master spy, the brilliant John Thurloe. Later, when in power, Thurloe controlled a network of listeners at doors, not only at home but throughout Europe, where there were hundreds of plots to overthrow Cromwell.

Thurloe, an ex-lawyer, became Home Secretary, Foreign Secretary, Secretary of State, Chief of Police, head of the Secret Service, War Secretary, Postmaster General and Councillor of States—all at the same time!—and with a huge budget purely for spying. Not bad! This meant total control, making his regime so tight that one of the Italian Council of Ten heard from the Venetian ambassador that, though England seemed completely up-to-date on what everyone else was doing, practically none of their own secrets ever escaped.

Thurloe did it by flashing wads of money at the Royalists abroad and at people in most of the foreign courts. "Good agents," he claimed, "cannot be gained but by money; for money they will do anything." Back in England, he divided the country into eleven districts, each policed by his own sort of militia. They intercepted practically every letter sent and offered cash rewards to anyone who'd snitch on their neighbors.

By the Way

The only reason Ollie Cromwell died peacefully in his bed was because Thurloe was totally aware of every single plot to kill him.

DEAD BUT HAPPY

John Churchill

Back in the seventeenth century, John Churchill, a supporter of the Royalists and the first duke of Marlborough, loved espionage and spent a fortune on it. He was famous for saying in defense of its great cost, "No war can be conducted successfully without early and good intelligence, and such advices cannot be had but at very great expense." He was obviously remembering the Battle of Sedgemoor in 1685, a typical good-news and bad-news scenario. The good news was that a spy told the rebel duke of Monmouth everything he needed to know about the royal army nearby. The bad news was that he forgot to mention a very deep, water-filled ditch that just happened to run between the two camps. When Monmouth's army attacked in the middle of the night, the Royalist army awoke to the sound of men splashing and cursing and promptly rushed out and beat them. The even-worse news was that poor old Monmouth lost his head a few days later.

Czar Paul of Russia

Catherine the Great's son Paul I took his mother's idea of a secret service one step further. He encouraged everyone in Russia to snitch on everyone else and put a big yellow box outside his palace where anyone from a road-sweeper to a high-ranking politician could drop in secret information about anyone. It got out of hand and so petty that one poor officer got a one-way ticket to the freezing wastes of Siberia simply for wearing his cap at the wrong angle. Anyway, the whole idea backfired as Czar Paul, obviously thinking his yellow box would at least keep him aware of plots and stuff, was assassinated in 1801 by a gang of his very own army officers. Apparently this had been the result of a huge plot dreamed up by nobles and military men who were fed up with the czar's increasingly silly behavior (and presumably his even sillier yellow box).

Duke of Wellington

Sir Arthur Wellesley, the duke of Wellington, the guy who beat Napoleon in 1815 (Battle of Waterloo), was a spymaster supreme. Wellington commented, "All the business of war is to find out what you don't know by what you do." He sent spies to find out everything about where a battle was likely to take place, what the enemy commanders were like, and how their troops were trained. He wanted to know what they got to eat and probably how often they went to the bathroom. He would even ask foreign locals what they thought about the British.

NOT INVENTED YET.

Charles Geneviève Louis August André Timothée d'Eon de Beaumont

If it wasn't bad enough having a mouthful like that for a name, young d'Eon (as we'll call him for short) was brought up by his mother to wear girl's clothes until his early teens. Helped by his pretty face and slight build, d'Eon slipped in and out of women's clothes at will and seemed to enjoy it (no comment!). But, strange as it might seem, d'Eon was no sissy. In fact, as well as having a law degree, he was considered a superb athlete and the most brilliant swordsman in all of France.

He was soon noticed by King Louis XV, who had his own little spying outfit (called Le Secret du Roi), and was asked to go on a strange mission. Using his ability to drop into girl's gear at the drop of a chapeau, he was sent to the court of the Czarina Elizabeth in Saint Petersburg, Russia, disguised as a young lady called Mademoiselle Lia de la Belmont. Oddly enough, the czarina herself liked to dress as a man. Is this all getting a bit weird? D'Eon or, should we say, Mademoiselle Lia was asked to find out (and did) just how close the Russians and the British were to putting together a joint army. If possible, he/she was to get them to favor France instead (French diplomats had been banned from Saint Petersburg for years). So far so good.

It worked like a charm. The czarina thought the girl was great and made Lia her maid of honor. All the French court painters wanted to paint the fresh new beauty in town, not guessing she was really a man. Gradually d'Eon, while

continually sending coded messages back home, managed to change Elizabeth's mind about the French and even to stop any idea she might have of signing a deal with the British. So far, so even better.

Eventually, the czarina was informed of the girl's secret and luckily was tickled pink, thinking it all quite funny. She even offered our hero a high rank in the Russian army, which he/she gracefully declined.

It had all gone so well that the young man returned to France in a blaze of glory with a pile of gold and a miniature portrait of the czarina herself. The French king was also delighted and presented him with a jewel-encrusted snuffbox. D'Eon was then made a permanent fixture in the French secret service. Things couldn't be better.

One of d'Eon's most famous spying jobs was when he was asked to come to England (as secretary to the French ambassador). The French planned to invade England. D'Eon's real job was to find out the best route to take once they landed. But all was not well back home. The king's dreadful new mistress, the infamous Madame de Pompadour, had always resented Louis's secret service and attempted to weed out its members and destroy them. D'Eon sat on top of her list. The mean madame tried to get him to come back to France, even stopping his pay when he refused. Her men then tried everything—poisoning, kidnapping, having him locked up in an asylum—you name it, but it was all to no avail.

It was when the old king died that things really came apart, however. D'Eon was broke and needed to get home. He wrote to the new king, Louis XVI, and told him that he was really a woman and that if Louis was anything like his dad he'd get the joke and send for him. Unfortunately, the new Louis didn't—and insisted that he must never dress as a French officer again, because it was an insult to France. He could come home, he conceded, but he must always be seen as a woman. Hmmm, tricky.

D'Eon was forced to agree but had his fingers crossed when he promised to obey. A little later, he was arrested in France for impersonating a French officer (and a man). They shipped him back to London where, to qualify for an allowance, he again had to dress as a woman for life. D'Eon got the short end of the stick completely, but Londoners found it entertaining. There were massive bets placed on whether or not he was indeed a man or a woman.

The rest of the story is so sad that it almost doesn't bear repeating. D'Eon was forced to remain as a woman for the rest of his life until his death in a cheap boardinghouse in 1810. He was eighty-three and poverty stricken. His landlady, undressing the withered "old lady" for her final trip (six feet under), was horrified to discover the answer to the riddle that had kept Londoners guessing for years.

Sidney Reilly

"Reckless Reilly," as he was known, was the spy to end all spies—the man who could have outwitted and out-womanized James Bond with both hands tied behind his back. He even looked a little like the movie star Humphrey Bogart. Reilly was actually born in Odessa, Russia, in 1874, not Ireland (as he claimed). His real dad had been a Jewish doctor in Vienna, not a Russian army colonel. This made him not Sidney Reilly but Sigmund Georgievich Rosenblum. Being Jewish in anti-Semitic Russia, as you can imagine, wasn't much fun, so young Sidney, Sigmund, or whatever you want to call him, decided to run for it. Sly Sid soon became the best kind of adventurer, popping up all over the world, using the many languages he spoke fluently. One time in the early 1890s, he even became the cook on the British expeditionary party that went up the Brazilian Amazon—no small feat in those days. It was on this particular outing that its leader, the well-known spymaster, Major Fothergill, noticed Sidney's many qualities and offered him a job in the British secret service.

So, in 1896, our Sidney became a real secret agent (a double agent even) working in the Far East for the British and the Japanese both at the same time (really Reilly!!).

By the Way

Sidney Reilly took his name (Reilly) from a wealthy widow named Margaret Reilly Thomas whose husband, the Reverend Hugh Thomas, Sidney kindly helped murder at the end of the century.

Later, in 1906, he turned up apparently working for the Russian czar, earning an amazingly fancy apartment in Saint Petersburg full of priceless old artwork. But all the time, he remained a special agent for the British. Basically Reilly searched the world to find the most trouble and got into it, working for whomever would pay the most. He had no fear. At one time during World War I, he parachuted behind German enemy lines. He stayed, pretending to be a perfect little German, and gathered secret information at the infamous weapons factory Krupp Works. Reilly killed two guards when he had to leave rather quickly. For this daring mission, he received Britain's Military Cross for bravery.

After the war, Reilly became obsessed with overturning the new Communist Soviet regime that had taken over Russia. He traveled in and out of Russia with a pass saying he was a member of the Soviet secret police.

It all came to a bad end (or didn't) in 1925, when Reilly was shot (or wasn't) trying to cross the Finnish border into Russia. Neither the Soviets nor the Brits would say anything about it—more than likely because they didn't know. Some say he was executed in 1925. Others say they saw him walking about, large as life, in 1927. Whether he was shot or really died or is even alive now (aged 135) will probably never be known. All we can assume is that Sidney Reilly kicked the bucket in the same manner as he lived—shrouded in deceit, in double-crossing, and in mystery. Whether Reilly was really working for the British or the Russians is probably the biggest mystery of all.

One thing is for certain, Sidney Sigmund Georgievich Rosenblum Reilly was the most celebrated spy of all time. He alone laid the foundation for the spy ring that eventually wriggled right into the heart of British society.

The Boy Scouts

Did you know that Robert Smyth, Lord Baden-Powell, the man who founded the Boy Scouts in 1908, was once a spy? Better still, did you know that Heinrich Himmler, who headed the Gestapo (Germany's secret police) during World War II, actually believed that because of

WHO ARE YOU — WORKING FOR?

this affiliation the scouts had to be a branch of the British secret service? I wonder what he thought the Girl Scouts and the Brownies were up to?

Baden-Powell was a whiz with the old paintbrush and, while sketching butterflies, integrated outlines of enemy fortifications or weapons into the complicated wing patterns and sent them home. Another trick he used was to soak his clothes in strong booze and totter off toward secret military installations. Having employed a good snoop, they'd usually find him but, because they thought a complete drunk was no threat to anyone, the sentries would just kick him out.

UNLIKELY SPIES

Prime Suspect, Geoffrey Prime

Can you imagine anywhere more innocent sounding than Laburnum Cottage, Pittville, Crescent Lane, Cheltenham? This was the home of Mr. Geoffrey Prime, a highly respectable rep for a wine company, and his wife. Little did the neighbors know of the real Mr. Prime.

On April 27, 1982, a couple of police officers called at the Primes' front door and asked whether Mr. Prime owned a two-tone, brown and cream Ford Cortina (a crime in itself). They wanted to find out why it had been seen in the same location as a series of assaults on young girls over the last couple of years. Prime denied knowing anything about it. After the police had gone, Prime broke down and confessed to his wife that he had committed the assaults. The good lady said she would support him through all the trials and tribulations ahead. Imagine her surprise, however, when having gotten all of that off of his chest, her hubby threw caution to the wind and confessed to having been a Soviet spy for the last fourteen years. I suppose he must have thought that having confessed to being a pervert, a spy wouldn't seem so bad.

The next day Prime went to the police and told all. Well almost all—he somehow forgot to mention the spying part. The shocked Mrs. Prime, waiting patiently at home, still didn't believe her old man had been a spy until she peeked into his briefcase (still on the hall table) and found, under a false bottom, a full set of spying tools—right down to a miniature camera, invisible-writing equipment, and a bunch of special little codebooks. After asking the advice of her priest, lawyer, and doctor (why not the milkman, I ask), she decided to spill the beans to the cops. Even the officer in charge didn't believe that the rather dorky looking Prime could possibly have been

such a dark and mysterious figure. But when he saw the old miniature spy equipment, he immediately called the police department's Special Branch, which arrived before he'd even put the phone down.

On further investigation, they found that Prime wasn't just a little man sending the odd piece of not-very-important stuff to the Soviets, but a big-time main agent dealing in the sort of secrets that made their eyes water.

Why Had He Dunnit?

Prime had been an unhappy loner as a kid and had been assaulted by an adult when very young. When he did his compulsory military training at eighteen, he was found to be good at languages, if not much else. Prime chose Russian, and, although turning out to be not as good as they at first thought, he did end up snooping on Russian voice transmissions at a Royal Air Force base in West Berlin, Germany. He was then promoted to sergeant.

When arrested for spying, Prime said that he'd gone over to the Soviets of his own accord. But it later looked much more probable that the Russkies had somehow discovered his unhealthy interest in young girls and had blackmailed him. They wanted to know how much the Brits knew of their operations and which codes they had already cracked. Prime tattled so well—and it pleased the Soviets so much—that he was sent to a special spy school at KGB headquarters in East Berlin, East Germany, where he was given a complete spy kit and, of course, money. It was all terribly ironic. While Prime was being checked out for an incredibly important security job in Britain (which he passed with flying colors), he was actually learning how to spy on them. What a joke!

His new British job required Prime to continue to listen in on top-secret Russian technical conversations and report what they were saying to British Intelligence. What he actually did was tell the Russians which of their lines of communication he was tapping so that they could pass lots of inaccurate hogwash to anyone listening. All this occurred in 1969, and Prime continued spying for years, despite being intensively examined six times by British Intelligence. He was so convincing that the British promoted him in 1975. He then found himself working among top-secret material that came over by satellite from the Central Intelligence Agency (CIA).

When eventually the KGB decided that Prime was of no further use, they cunningly decided to throw him to the wolves by wining and dining him in public with well-known Soviet agents at top Viennese restaurants. They hoped that the British agents known to use the same places would spot Prime and then handle the situation in the usual way. But although the Russkies flaunted him in all the fanciest hotels and restaurants, they weren't spotted once by the British agents. Prime worked for another two years before being arrested, as we now know, on a pure fluke.

The Special Branch originally considered him a sad, inadequate, perverted man. Shocked, they realized he was an incredibly clever and important Soviet agent who, during his time, removed, photographed, and passed on countless top-secret documents. Geoffrey Prime was sentenced to thirty-five years for spying and a further three for indecent assault on children.

Sir Anthony Blunt

Here is the headline news from November 20, 1979.

A shocked House of Commons heard today that the queen's distinguished art adviser and friend, Sir Anthony Blunt, 72, is a Russian spy. He was the notorious fourth man in the famous Burgess, Maclean, and Philby affair whom all the secret services had been trying to track down for years. Sir Anthony will, of course, be immediately stripped of his knighthood.

This was the final link in a story that had intrigued the world of espionage for years. It all began back in 1926 at Cambridge University, when the young, gawky, idealistic, but nonetheless brilliant, vicar's son (not to mention relative of the late Queen Mother) became a tutor as soon as he'd finished his studies. At that time, a lot of the fashionable Cambridge undergrads were carried away with the idea that Britain, the United States, and Western Europe were sliding farther into the hideous world of capitalism. These undergrads

AH JENKINS — I THINK I MIGHT HAVE A LITTLE JOB FOR YOU.

wanted these countries to follow the bleak path of Communist Russia. Blunt was the first recruited by the Russians in 1933, and his first convert was Guy Burgess. This pair became part of the "Ring of Five," perhaps the most famous spy ring ever organized by the KGB. Their first job was to help the Russians stop the Nazis, who were making warlike noises in Germany. Blunt and Burgess recruited Donald Maclean, the lesser-known American, Michael Straight, and lastly Kim Philby. Blunt's main job was to spot anyone else among the undergrads who might want to do the same sort of thing (and cheat on their country at the same time).

It was totally bizarre that Blunt was accepted by MI5 (Britain's counterintelligence bureau) in 1939 at the beginning of World War II, especially when you consider that he had been a fully paid-up Communist in earlier life. But accepted he was, and he proceeded to wreck MI6's (Britain's secret service) counterespionage efforts abroad without anyone having any idea what he was up to. He also let his Soviet bosses know exactly who was sending secrets to Britain and gave them names and addresses of everyone who worked for MI5. When he became in charge of surveillance (spy watching), he was finally able to tell his Soviet bosses exactly who was watching whom, where and when, whichever side they were on. Anthony Blunt was actually the perfect spy.

All through this period, Blunt managed to keep his job as deputy director of the very cool Courtauld Institute of Art. He even met his spymates in his London office, using the office's equipment to copy important documents that he sent on to Russia. A lot of the stuff he sent—regarding the exact location of the soon-to-be-happening Normandy landings, for example—would have cost thousands of Allied lives had his Soviet bosses acted on it.

Blunt left MI5 after the war to be the incredibly important Surveyor of Pictures for King George VI. This provided excellent cover for his other new job as messenger boy for Soviet spies, at the same time giving them any information he could wheedle out of his old colleagues in MI5. Things eventually became hot for Blunt, when his old college friends Burgess and Maclean escaped to Russia. He refused to go himself, purely because working for Buckingham Palace was such an easy task. Despite being interrogated by the British intelligence services practically every five minutes, (they were sure he must be up to something), he continued to pass messages to and fro for years.

In 1963 the game was suddenly up, when a former Soviet spy working oddly enough as President John Kennedy's art adviser, suddenly confessed all and named Blunt as the agent who'd recruited him. Amazingly, Blunt was told that if he spilled the beans, naming names and explaining codes, they wouldn't prosecute him. Odd. Anyone else would have received execution for high treason. It's thought that his high-up royal connections saved him. For whatever reasons, it appears that Blunt did confess all.

Or did he? All the information he gave under oath appears to have been a bunch of lies designed to throw the British off the real track. Either way, his lurid career seemed to have been forgotten. Years later he was even knighted for work carried out for—get ready—MI5!

In 1983 a book came out telling the whole sorry story of Burgess, Maclean, and, much more to the point, Blunt. This time the game was up for good, and the country was after his traitorous hide. Blunt, at the age of seventy-six, died broken and alone in 1983, a disgrace to all who knew him.

Ian Fleming

You'd never think that the guy who created James Bond knew a lot about real espionage, would you? You'd be wrong. Not only did Ian Fleming know a lot about it, he'd been in it up to his suave and sophisticated neck for most of his working life—before deciding to write. Not only that, but our Ian was a lot like Mr. Bond himself.

Son of wealthy parents, a playboy around London, and bored with life as a stockbroker, young Ian craved excitement. He eventually met someone in the British naval intelligence, who was looking for bright young guys who were prepared to do just about anything as long as it was dangerous and the

money was good. Fleming was perfect—mad as a hatter, brave as a bulldog, and with ideas galore.

Fleming's first solo job, during World War II, was for Room 39 (his department's nickname) and involved Rudolf Hess (deputy leader of the Nazi Party). Fleming believed that if he could get one of the Nazis' top men to defect to Britain, it would strike fear into the Germans. He chose the infamous Hess purely because of his one weakness, he was deeply into astrology (star signs). Fleming managed to get in touch with the two Swiss astrologers often used by high-ranking German officers. Fleming told them to tell Hess that his big moment of truth was near—he'd been chosen by the fickle finger of fate to go to Britain and smoke big pipe of peace with Britain's prime minister, Winston Churchill. This, without any doubt, would make him the greatest and most popular man in the whole wide world. In 1941 Hess swallowed the bait big time. He borrowed a Messerschmitt fighter and flew it to Scotland, where he ordered the somewhat awestruck local police to take him to their leader.

Oh dear, instead of being delighted, the British government, including Mr. Churchill, saw him not only as an embarrassment but as potentially dangerous. They were worried that he might shine a torch on all the high-up Britons (including the king's brother, the duke of Windsor), who'd been having cozy fireside chats with the top German leader, Adolf Hitler. The government, therefore, let it be known that Hess was a total loony and no use to man nor beast. Hess went to jail and stayed there until he died in 1989.

By the Way

Hitler went crazy when the story got out and had every single clairvoyant, astrologer, or fortune-teller arrested. Their craft, art, or whatever you might call it, was banned in Germany.

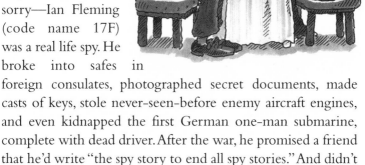

James Bond—sorry—Ian Fleming (code name 17F) was a real life spy. He broke into safes in foreign consulates, photographed secret documents, made casts of keys, stole never-seen-before enemy aircraft engines, and even kidnapped the first German one-man submarine, complete with dead driver. After the war, he promised a friend that he'd write "the spy story to end all spy stories." And didn't he do well!

The Real James Bond

Everyone's heard of James Bond. In fact, some people would find it difficult to name another spy. But did anyone like him really exist? Legend has it that he was just a huge mishmash of all the agents Ian Fleming had ever met—with a great dollop of idealism thrown in. "M," on the other hand, was really a guy called Maxwell Knight, onetime boss of MI5 and a brilliant spy catcher. Fleming got the idea of the one letter name from a guy called Vernon Kell—code name "Major K."

The British secret services were born in 1909. Bond's forerunners consisted of a three-officer outfit. Their back-up team included a secretary, a cleaning lady, and a simple motto: "Trust no one." Since World War I, the number of agents rose to ten. But however amateur the British had been, the German agents were even worse. Practically all their devices and tricks were known by the British.

The dashing, one-man hit squad that was James Bond did not exist, nor did anyone remotely like him. Apart from anything else, if his hazardous lifestyle hadn't killed him, his self-indulgence would have. It's been calculated that he'd have slept with over seventy women a year, smoked seventy unfiltered black Russian cigarettes a day, and drunk enough martinis (shaken not stirred) to kill a bar full of people. He was licensed to kill all right—himself!!

The Krogers

As a kid, I sometimes rode my bike down Cranley Drive in the boring London suburb of Ruislip near my childhood home. I must have passed number 45 when the Krogers lived there. So what? I hear you cry. The Krogers turned out to be a couple of the most famous Soviet spies ever to live in Britain. And 45 Cranley Drive became the headquarters of one of the most infamous Communist spy rings run by one of Russia's cleverest agents. But why Ruislip? Easy! Because nothing ever happens there! Brilliant! Back to the plot.

Nobody noticed the well-dressed, good-looking man with the small briefcase who visited the dull-as-dishwater Krogers every few weeks for supper. He was Konon Molody (Gordon Lonsdale).

Gordon Lonsdale/Konon Molody

Comrade Molody was a famous Soviet war hero who could speak practically every language backward. He was asked to spy on Britain—a great honor. His controllers wanted to know all about British and American airbases. (By the way, did I forget to mention there was a huge American base at West Ruislip?)

In 1955, disguised as a Canadian businessman and carrying the passport of a certain missing Gordon Lonsdale, Konon Molody arrived in Britain. Lonsdale/Molody set up several lucrative businesses, including supplying stuff like jukeboxes and bubblegum machines to places like airbases (fancy that). He even invented a car burglar alarm that won him the coveted Gold Medal at the Brussels International Trade Fair for the best British entry. With all that and the money he received from the Soviets, he was soon spending cash like it was going out of style. This tended to make one rather popular in the 1950s (or any time, come to think of it). It didn't take long before the very best people began to appear at his ritzy, no-expense-spared parties. Under the cover of his businesses, the suave, handsome company director traveled the country, but his real purpose was to make friends with anyone who had anything to do with weapons or intelligence organizations.

It was in this way that Lonsdale met the Krogers, Russian agents who'd fled from the United States when they were about to be uncovered. In their house on Cranley Drive, they had a full set of spying equipment right down to a radio that could connect with anywhere in the world. Lonsdale used them to send all his snippets of information back home to the old country (i.e., the Soviet Union).

This all went along just fine until Lonsdale met Harry Houghton—then it went even finer. Okay, Houghton was a secretary, but it was where he was a secretary that was important. He worked at the top-secret Admiralty Underwater Weapons Establishment in southern England. The KGB had dug around and found out that the otherwise colorless clerk had been somewhat of a bad boy in early life—selling stuff on the black market during the war. This information, admittedly not high profile, was enough to make him highly corruptible or at least blackmailable.

Lonsdale, now calling himself Commander Alex Johnson from the U.S. Embassy, soon discovered that Houghton would do practically anything for money, especially for untraceable cash. Johnson tricked Houghton into believing that he was getting all the secret stuff for Britain's U.S. allies. Soon the most classified top-secret information about the British navy and docks was winging its way over the airwaves from Cranley Drive—not to America but to Moscow.

Eventually, Houghton's lifestyle gave him away. How could a man on secretary's income afford a new car and an expensive new house, not to mention the lifestyle to go with it? MI5 put him under surveillance and watched all the swapping-of-bags-in-public-places routines between Houghton and Lonsdale.

Lonsdale was on the hook, and he led his shadows to his bank, where he casually deposited a small brown case. It contained a miniature Russian camera, a magnifying glass (so he could see the camera?), and a bunch of assorted keys.

From then on, it was easy. Lonsdale soon showed the British agents the way to Ruislip, but, cleverly, they didn't swoop down immediately. They wanted the big catch. It came on January 7, 1961, three months later. Under full surveillance, Houghton and his girlfriend, Bunty Gee, arrived at a London train station, carrying a large shopping bag. There they met Lonsdale. As they swapped bags, detectives from

Special Branch nabbed them. The bag contained four top-secret files and over 300 photos of plans of Britain's ever-so-secret nuclear submarines.

Then it was back to Ruislip and the Krogers. They at first denied everything . . . until even the most simple search revealed an Aladdin's cave of spying equipment and best (or worst) of all, under the floorboards, a device for sending coded messages at a rate of 200 words a minute. They were caught red-handed, and so was Lonsdale, and so was Houghton, and so was Bunty Gee.

What Happened to Them All?

Lonsdale got twenty-five years in jail, but upon receiving the sentence laughed out loud. He knew that in no time he would be swapped for one of Britain's imprisoned agents in Russia—which he was. Houghton and Gee got fifteen years each, and the Krogers got twenty.

The Undercover Pope

Giovanni Montini was a very ambitious man. He entered the Catholic Church in 1920 and soon had his eye on the top job—pope. The super-keen young novice turned out to be an absolute whiz at organization. It was no surprise that, by 1937, he'd reached dizzying heights in the Vatican (the pope's headquarters) and was hobnobbing with the actual pope, Pius XII. The Vatican, by the way, was to have an important role during World War II, acting as a go-between for all the different countries involved.

Anyway, Montini soon had his fingers in absolutely everything and was nicknamed "the man who knows all and sees all." He did indeed know everyone from diplomats to businesspeople to politicians. This meant that, if anyone wanted to have words with the Vatican, they had to go through Giovanni—no kidding! By the time he'd made bishop, he'd become the only choice to set up the newfangled Vatican Information Service—a polite term for an undercover

intelligence agency. But when the war began, Montini refused to take sides and wouldn't give away any secrets to either side.

Enter James Jesus Angleton, head of counterespionage for the Italian government. This chain-smoking Yale graduate knocked on Montini's door asking about an undercover agent, codename VESSEL. The agent seemed to be getting amazing information out of the highly secretive Vatican and was passing it on to the Americans. Angleton wondered if all this stuff was true or some load of junk supplied by the Russians or the Japanese, in order to deceive the British? The Americans were sure it was okay, however, and had refused to question it.

Montini soon corrected Angleton, saying that the information was nonsense and had nothing to do with what was discussed at top Vatican meetings. But there still remained the questions of who was doing it, why he was doing it, and who he was working for.

It turned out that there was just one guy behind the whole silly business. VESSEL turned out to be Virgilio Scattolini, a journalist and ex-pornographer who, having seen the Catholic light, packed up his seedy profession and ended up writing for the Vatican's own newspaper. When the editor found out exactly what Scattolini had been up to before joining his paper, he fired him. This miffed Scattolini a great deal, so he simply continued selling his own made-up Vatican "secrets" from outside the Vatican walls. Well, that is until Angleton and Montini stopped him.

The two men were suddenly pitched into the spotlight. Together they used their skills to organize the surrender of all the Germans and Italians in northern Italy, saving thousands of lives and the country from total destruction.

As for Giovanni, he went on to become archbishop of Milan. In 1963 the undercover wheeler-dealer became Pope Paul VI. He died in 1978, but his promotion might not have even stopped there, as there is talk about making him a saint—which is about as far as you can get.

Les Brown—Who?

In July 1983, helicopters and ships spent a long weary night trying to locate a lonely SOS bleep. In France, radar operators managed to pin the signal down to the Firth of Clyde in Scotland. The Faslane nuclear submarine base did much better and finally homed in on—get ready—a humble house near Glasgow. Fisherman Les Brown, sound asleep in bed with his wife, had left a radio distress beacon on top of the wardrobe. The device was apparently faulty and still giving out a weak signal. The vastly expensive air and sea hunt ended with poor Les being woken up by a helicopter pilot and a police officer hammering on his front door.

No great harm done, you might think. Unfortunately, a Soviet spy satellite picked up the signal first. Its ability to isolate such a tiny object shocked the Soviet-watchers in the West. If they could detect that faint signal, what else could they see? Not that the West had anything to complain about, as it turned out. Only a few weeks later, a couple of Russian jets caused an international incident by shooting down a perfectly innocent Korean airliner that had strayed into Soviet air space. They would have gotten away with the disaster had the Americans not been watching Russia's every move on their own highly sophisticated surveillance satellites.

WOMEN SPIES

Although Russia's famous spymaster Richard Sorge said that ladies would always be "unfit for espionage work," spying has always been one of the few professions with equal opportunities for women. This is probably because they are generally regarded as more trustworthy than men (please debate?). Here are a few of the most famous.

Aphra Behn

Despite her rather exotic name, Aphra Behn was probably Britain's first female spy, dating back to the seventeenth century. She married a Dutch merchant and, because of that fact, gained specialized knowledge of Holland and the Dutch (who at that time were always threatening to invade Britain).

Unfortunately, in those days, women weren't taken very seriously, so when she sent back secret messages from Holland claiming that the Dutch had rebuilt their navy and were simply dying to try it out, the poor lady was ignored. They should have listened. In 1667 a bunch of Dutch fire ships sailed right up the Thames River and brazenly destroyed the British fleet.

Louise de Kéroualle

The beautiful Louise was sent by Louis XIV of France to find out what the British were really thinking during negotiations for the Treaty of Dover in 1670. There were two treaties being ironed out. One (which was top secret) had to do with Britain's Charles II agreeing to allow Britain to convert to Catholicism (for lots of money and 6,000 French troops). The other, more formal one was about Britain supporting the French against Holland (for which Charles would get even more money). The French king chose Louise de Kéroualle, not only because she was gorgeous but because he knew she

was the kind of woman Britain's king really liked. She therefore acted as bait for King Charles, who predictably swallowed the plot hook, line, and sinker. He not only took her to his bedroom but made her the duchess of Portsmouth. They even conceived one of his many children between horse races at Newbury. I bet you didn't know that!

Lydia Darragh

During the American Revolution (1775–1783), General George Washington had to use the sneakiest of tactics to fight the British, from whom the Americans were trying to break away. At that time, Britain

was the most powerful nation in the world. Among Washington's many stunts, he had his troops dress up as British soldiers, go behind the enemy lines, and attack them from the rear (ouch!). He also allowed false documents to get stolen by British spies and even had fake forts built simply to fool the enemy.

But Washington was known best of all for his gathering of enemy intelligence and was even given a special secret fund for that purpose alone. Top of the spy pile was a quiet middle-class lady named Lydia Darragh, probably the most unlikely spy ever.

Respectable Lydia Darragh lived with her respectable husband (Mr. Darragh) at 177 South Second Street in the respectable city of Philadelphia, Pennsylvania. Both were devout Quakers and hated wars but not, as it happened, the individual soldiers who fought in them.

When the British took over Philadelphia, the officers seized all of the best houses (including the Darraghs') for themselves. As Lydia's had the biggest parlor, the Brits chose it for their strategy meetings. This decision, as you might imagine, really upset the peace-loving couple. The officers had no reason to suspect the polite, butter-wouldn't-melt-in-her-mouth, sweet-faced lady in the gray dress who took their coats as they arrived. But dear Mrs. Darragh was not quite as innocent as she appeared.

For months she used her fourteen-year-old son John as a courier, passing snippets of intelligence to her eldest son Charles, a lieutenant in Washington's army. Most of the time, the information was pretty small stuff (important, but nothing to win or lose major battles). Then one night, the officers suggested that she and her family go to bed early. Something big was afoot, and now-nosy Lydia wanted to know about it.

Listening outside the door in her curlers and stockinged feet, Mrs. Darragh not only found out that the British were finally about to attack Washington's army. She also learned just how big their army was (5,999 men) and what equipment they had (thirteen cannons etc.). The British officers then, to her horror, actually announced the night of the attack (only two days away), which would, of course, make for a complete surprise—not to mention massacre.

In the morning, having boldly received a pass from the Brits to go over enemy lines (she said she needed to collect flour from the local mill), Lydia scuttled off to get this scary news off her chest. She eventually reached the American army and spilled the beans—big time—to the shocked officers. Needless to say, when the British marched on Washington's camp, the Americans were so ready for them that the Brits didn't even bother to take the attack any further and turned around and retreated.

Nobody ever suspected Lydia or her family. No hint was ever mentioned officially or in any war reports. American historians, however, hail Lydia Darragh as a true heroine, whose bravery contributed to the successful struggle for American independence from Britain.

Emma Edmonds

Some women got so caught up in causes that they chopped off their hair and enlisted in armies as men. One of these women was Sarah Emma Edmonds, who enlisted in the Second Michigan Infantry as Franklin Thompson in the Civil War (1861–1865).

The daughter of a grumpy Canadian potato farmer, Emma was born in 1839. She never went to school because she had to work in the fields (picking grumpy Canadian potatoes). When she was eighteen, her dad announced he'd chosen a husband for her. She promptly dressed from head to toe as a man and left. (I guess she didn't go for her dad's choice.) When next we hear of Emma, she'd set up a successful business as a traveling Bible sales "man." Emma's wanderings brought her back to visit her old hometown, where only the family dog (name unknown) recognized her. Glad to say, he didn't snitch.

SHHH!

HE SMELLS FAMILIAR

It was around this time that Miss Edmonds (still dressed as a man) rented a room in the house of a Methodist minister who also headed the local militia. He suggested to "Franklin Thompson" (the name Emma was using) that he join the battalion when the Civil War broke out in 1861. Franklin/Emma agreed.

After leaving the army, Emma wrote of her adventures in a book called *Nurse and Spy in the Union Army*. She'd tended the sick and carried messages to and fro on the battlefield. She's remembered, however, for the "spy" part of the title.

To do the spy part, she exchanged her uniform for the gear of an African slave who toiled on the plantations of the Confederate States (the South). She cropped her hair real close, and then, with a bottle of silver nitrate, stained her head, face, hands, and feet black. She was so convincing that she passed through the rebel lines without attracting a second glance. She joined up with a bunch of slaves who were delivering coffee and food to the troops. Even these slaves didn't smell a rat (or a woman).

Emma was then singled out and shoved into a work gang of black male slaves, who were ordered to build fortifications at a Confederate base. After her torturingly hard day's work, she strolled around the base, making notes and tucking them into the soles of her shoes. After many adventures, she escaped back to the Union army and was taken directly to General George McClellan's headquarters to tell him what she'd learned. Emma eventually returned to her home, changed into a woman again, and married a local man.

Later, in 1884, a middle-aged woman applied for an army pension. At first, they couldn't get it into their heads that she was the same Franklin Thompson, but eventually they believed her and awarded her a pension "for her sacrifices in the line of duty, her splendid record as a soldier, her unblemished character, and disabilities incurred in the service."

HONEST SIR! I USED TO BE A MAN!

Mata Hari

Margaretha Geertruida Zelle was the daughter of a rich and reportedly bad-tempered Dutch hatter. She became the most famous, the most mysterious, and the sexiest lady spy in history. She began her career as Lady McLeod, a cross between a belly dancer and a common stripper. She'd taken her name from her husband, Captain Rudolph McLeod. She had separated from the mean drunk just before reaching Paris in 1905. There she told everyone that her name was Mata Hari ("eye of the morning") and that she was the product of an Indian holy man and a temple dancer who'd died at her birth. Miss Hari quickly became famous throughout the nightclubs of Paris because of her willingness to dance practically nude at the drop of a hat. She also befriended any man who paid her enough money. Her best claim to fame, however, came during World War I, when she toured Europe, seducing high-ranking officers on both sides, French or German, and then selling their pillow talk to their respective enemies.★

Actually, if truth be told, Mata Hari was never that beautiful, and the secrets weren't often of much value. I mean, who really wants to know what a German general wears to bed? But that really wasn't the point. When the French realized, in 1917, that she'd been working for both sides at once and that neither side trusted her further than they could throw her, they arrested and tried her for treason. Her foolish explanation of why one single German officer paid her a huge sum of money was the last straw. She told the court, apparently, that it was the going rate for the pleasure of her company. They replied by letting her know that the going rate for treason was the firing squad.

Leonora Heinz

Leonora Heinz was a rather plain, rather lonely German girl who lived by herself in a chic apartment in Bonn, Germany. On March 1, 1960, she opened her front door to a good-looking young man called Heinz Suetterlin. Handsome Heinz carried a bunch of roses and said he was answering a lonely hearts advertisement. Leonora told him that he'd made a mistake, for she'd never advertised. But—let's face it (she must've thought)—how many times had she had such an opportunity knock on her door—and a single opportunity as

★*The Germans even sent her to a how-to-be-a-spy school in Belgium.*

well! She promptly asked him in for a cup of coffee. Bad move number one, Leonora!

Suetterlin had been trained to perfection in the art of seduction. He learned from Soviet spymasters who had built whole training camps full of fancy restaurants, bars, and cinemas to imitate the cities of the West. Here young Soviet studs (called ravens) and women (called swans) were schooled in Western ways and particularly in how to charm the pants off important targets.

But why poor Miss Heinz? Well, surprise, surprise, she just happened to work as a secretary in the West German government's foreign ministry. They targeted her purely and cynically because undercover agents had spotted just how desperate she seemed for a man. It was a well-known fact that most of those extremely well-off young women employed by the West Germans had just about everything they could desire—except men.

Smoothy Suetterlin made Leonora Heinz fall head-over-heels in love with him. The love-stricken girl had no choice when he threatened to leave her if she didn't bring home top-secret documents from work. She was putty in his hands. Most lunchtimes, she rushed home from work to cook the lazy Suetterlin his lunch (beans on toast), while he copied the stuff that she'd brought back in a special false-bottomed handbag (a present from Russia).

In six years, she supplied over 3,000 documents, some of them reeking of stupendous military importance. The couple sent them to the KGB before the ink was hardly dry. At one stage, the Soviets were even reading documents and messages before the German foreign minister got a chance.

The couple were eventually arrested. Poor Leonora realized the ghastly truth that her now-husband not only didn't love her but didn't even like her—and never had. She hung herself that very night in her cell.

DEADLY SPIES

When someone in the twilight world of espionage becomes a problem, it often becomes necessary to, how shall we say . . . dispense with his or her services . . . um, permanently. This could be either because they know too much, because their services are no longer required, or because they've been found working for the enemy. In the past, most intelligence organizations have employed real hitmen, whose job is to get rid of anyone they're asked to, as quickly and as silently as possible—no questions asked. The nickname for this operation in the spy world is a "wet affair."

Here are a few of the most famous incidents throughout history (the ones that are known about, that is).

Nikolai Khokhlov

Nikolai Khokhlov was a well-known Soviet spymaster who had sent lots of his people into non-Communist Europe to get rid of so-called enemies of the state. One day in 1954, he was "asked" to do the dirty deed himself. His target was Georgi Okolovich, a fervent anti-Communist who lived in Frankfurt, Germany. It was good timing, because Khokhlov had long been looking for a way to escape to the joys of hamburgers and Coca-Cola in the United States. He decided to spare his victim and used him to get in touch with American agents. To prove he was who he was, he showed the American agents some of his special gizmos, including his latest Soviet weapon, a gold cigarette case that doubled as a nifty electric pistol, shooting deadly dumdum bullets tastily coated in cyanide.

His former Soviet bosses were understandably annoyed and decided to teach him a lesson. In September 1957, Khokhlov collapsed while talking at a Frankfurt meeting. He was rushed to a hospital, but they couldn't find the antidote to the poison he'd obviously been given. By this time, dark brown blotches and black-and-blue swellings covered poor old Nikolai. Blood actually seeped through his skin. His hair then parted company with his head in great black tufts. Worse still, his bones began to decay, and his blood started turning to water—he really wasn't well at all. The doctors eventually figured out that he'd been poisoned with the drug thallium, which had been exposed to atomic radiation (definitely something you don't want on your cornflakes). Poor old Khokhlov miraculously survived but remained bald as an egg and covered in hideous scars.

Georgi Markov

Georgi Markov was a Communist playwright who'd defected to Britain from Bulgaria and persisted in writing stuff that really got to the Soviet chiefs back home. One day, while waiting for a London bus, he felt a sharp prick in his leg. He whipped around to see a man picking up an umbrella nearby. The man said he was sorry and jumped into a taxi, which sped away. Markov thought nothing of it and went home to his wife and supper. Later, while watching television, he began to feel a bit sick. After another four days, he was stone cold dead, but none of the hospital doctors could trace the cause. At the post-mortem, however, they found a tiny little platinum ball embedded in his leg. It had been drilled and filled with ricin, a drug twice as powerful as cobra venom and with no known antidote. Experts believe it had been fired from a special miniature surgical device hidden in the umbrella's tip.

Buster Crabb

I remember this name because his disappearance in 1956 caused massive headlines throughout the Western world. Nikolai Bulganin and Nikita Khrushchev, the mighty Soviet leaders, had sailed to Britain to try, once and for all, to calm down the Cold War between the East and the West. They warned the British to keep away from their boat—the very latest in Soviet warships—which bristled with secret weapons and everything. Even Britain's new prime minister, Sir Anthony Eden, told MI5 and MI6 to keep away from the ship and the two Soviets. But naval intelligence simply didn't believe that was what he really wanted, and they couldn't bear having such a prize in their waters without being able to take a look around. They decided Eden would actually be delighted if they found out a lot of secret stuff about the Soviet boat.

The navy promptly set up radar on the cliffs of Dover so as to keep an eye on it and even made sure that Bulganin and Khrushchev's rooms in a high-end London hotel were fully bugged. Better still, they went for an idea first suggested by top war hero and experienced frogman Commander "Buster" Crabb. He suggested he dive under the ship's hull to have a good look around.

Heads You Lose

After the dive, poor Buster, a short, hairy, thickset man, was never seen again. Or was he? Some witnesses reported that they'd seen a group of Soviet frogmen wrestling with a lone frogman before dragging him onto their ship. A year later, however, a headless, handless body wearing the same type of frogman's outfit as Crabb's was found nearby and identified by Crabb's widow as her husband (I suppose she should have known—head, hands, or not). Case closed? Not quite.

As soon as the news hit the headlines, however, a Soviet sailor reported that the Russkies had nabbed Crabb and that he was safe and sound (complete with his limbs and head) in a Soviet jail. Then the Soviet government claimed that Crabb had actually gone over to their side of his own free will. They even produced a remarkably convincing photo of him dressed as a Soviet sailor.

The real story will probably never be known, but it's thought that Soviet spies had gotten wind of Crabb's plan to snoop around their precious warship and were down there waiting for him in a special little underwater compartment. They had probably dealt with him then and there in the way they knew best, so it looks like he lost his head after all. Either way, members of the British government ended up with oodles of egg on their, as it turned out, maybe innocent faces.

TOOLS OF THE TRADE

Let's imagine that you're a real spy. For all I know, you might be (the oddest people read my books). If you are, don't bother to read this chapter; you should know it all. The rest of you might like to know about the tools for successful spying, just in case. Here are a few of the absolute essentials.

Pigeons

Some people think that racing pigeons only live in sheds in people's backyards, but actually the clever birds have helped send secret messages, as far back as Roman times. Before World War I, however, using pigeons as a method of passing messages had kind of died out. But naval intelligence still used them extensively when the radio wouldn't work. The Brits even had a field intelligence division that used high-flying reconnaissance balloons to relay information quickly. Each carried a couple of pigeons. Right up to the end of World War II, in fact, Britain called on a "pigeon post" if no other method was available.

On July 30, 1942, the Royal Society for the Prevention of Cruelty to Animals gave a special award to Mercury for a special record-breaking flight. The daring bird flew 480 miles, without stopping for breakfast, lunch, or dinner. Across enemy lands and over the bleak North Sea, it carried an important message from a Danish resistance group on its leg. Over a hundred British birds had been parachuted in crates, but

WHY CAN'T THEY USE THE BLASTED PHONE?

only Mercury returned. I bet the rest defected and their descendants are probably living in complete luxury in Germany.

Invisible Ink

All spies have to pass messages between each other, and it's probably better that other people don't read them. Invisible ink provides one of the easiest methods, and there are many ways of making it. One of the best and simplest methods is to mix a little alum (aluminum sulphate) with water. You can then write using a pointed stick or an old-fashioned dip pen. When the ink dries, you can see nothing (apart from the paper, of course). Should you run a hot iron over it, however, the message will be revealed loud and clear. The trouble is that anyone opening an envelope to find a piece of paper with absolutely nothing on it might smell a rat. The answer is simple. Write a second message in pencil over the invisible one and tell your fellow conspirator to erase it before ironing the paper.

By the Way

If you think my method wouldn't work, listen to this. Whenever Germans were captured, the number of lemons they carried puzzled their captors. It was later discovered that they wrote messages in lemon juice over the normal ink ones.

By Another Way

The better-equipped German spies soaked their ties and socks with chemicals to be used later for invisible ink. When they got to their lodgings in Britain, they squeezed the items in distilled water, and presto, they were ready to write.

A World of Gadgets

Size is everything . . . the smaller the better in this case. Ian Fleming, for instance, favored a tiny cyanide gun disguised as a fountain pen. Others prefer dummy cigarette packs that kill (slightly faster than the usual contents) by firing poison darts. Also on your shopping list could be a watch that tells you exactly where you are in the world or shoes that have deadly retractable needles, etc. etc. The most important gadgets to any real spy are bugs—not the creepy-crawly kind, but tiny electronic listening devices planted somewhere in the enemy camp and designed to relay every word.

Bugs Abounding

Probably the biggest bugging operation ever cropped up in 1968 when the Americans and the Soviets agreed to build embassies in each other's countries. This was a nice friendly idea but potentially a little risky. The Russkies, suspicious as ever, employed one security expert to every two workers while building theirs in New York. The far more trusting Americans in Moscow just let the Soviets handle constructing it. Surprise, surprise, when they came to examine the finished building, they found lots of bugs—the place was riddled with 'em. The Soviets had mixed tiny microphones into the very concrete that built the walls—making them impossible to get rid of without pulling down the whole place. The Americans simply added three more floors to the top of the building at a cost of $40 million. Job done? Well, um . . . perhaps not. The architect they eventually chose turned out to be a Soviet spy. Whoops!

Codes and Ciphers

Secret codes go back many years. Religious writers sometimes hid what they were saying by reversing the alphabet (using the last letter of the alphabet instead of the first and so on). Greek generals went for the old parchment around the staff trick, while the Greek writer Polybius invented the 5 x 5 square pic, which is the basis of so many cryptographic (code) systems. Another method simply advanced each letter of the alphabet five places, a system used by Julius Caesar that is called the Caesar Shift.

Although it is believed that there is no such thing as an uncrackable code, the very best codes take so long to unravel that by the time they are, they are usually of no use. The Chinese have always relied heavily on memory for their secret messages, tending to keep actual coding to a minimum. This actually has more to do with their complicated writing system than anything else. Lately, however, they've taken to using the Roman alphabet.

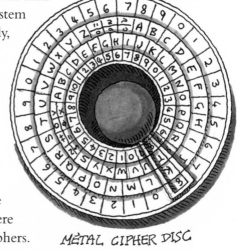

In Europe, the use of codes and ciphers in spy circles is as popular today as it was in the Middle Ages. Up until World War I, the most popular codes were usually "substitution" ciphers. Briefly, cracking them involved

METAL CIPHER DISC
1802

comparing how often certain letters turned up in a hidden message compared to how often they'd turn up naturally in that particular language. Although somewhat difficult to figure out in those days, a fairly ordinary computer could sort them out in minutes. This is why Britain's decoding center at Government Communications Headquarters in Cheltenham has the most extensive computer system in Europe.

One of the great breakthroughs in coding cropped up in 1976. Adi Shamir, an Israeli mathematician, invented a way of writing to his friend Leonard Aldeman at the University of Southern California that only he could possibly understand. I won't attempt to explain it (on account of I can't understand it), but it involved the use of large prime numbers (those numbers that can only be divided by themselves and the number one). By a system of multiplication, a set of numbers could be achieved that could only be deciphered by someone who already knew certain secret prime numbers. Clear? It is thought that even the most clever computer in the world would take years to decipher the code. Even if it did succeed, it would only take a couple of hours for the cunning codesters to put the machine right back to where it started.

Enigma

During World War II, the Germans invented the Enigma Cryptograph. Despite looking like a cross between a shoe box and an old-fashioned cash register, this compact machine scrambled messages until they read like pure German gobbledygook. There were over 150 million, million, million different settings, and these were changed practically every day. The codes they spewed out became so complex that only a sister Enigma machine could understand what they were talking about. A brilliant team of British codebreakers worked day and night for ages to crack its funny talk, but to no avail. It was only when an actual Enigma machine was stolen and smuggled back to Britain (luckily with an instruction manual showing all the settings) that the British were able to figure out what the Germans were up to. This factor alone shortened the war by a good few years. When, however, the Nazis realized that the British were on to them, they changed all the settings (typical!). It took another huge team of top mathematicians and puzzlers a whole year to crack the pesky codes again.

By the Way

On April 2, 2000, a priceless Enigma machine was stolen from the museum at Bletchley Park, where the code-breaking team had worked. It seems rather ironic that a building that has been so involved with national security has only just begun to install its own security system.

By Another Way

After the war, in what looked like a kindly act, Britain and America sold off their old reconditioned Enigma machines to smaller countries at silly prices, urging them to use them for their most secret communications. How thoughtful? Not at all. All this meant was that the British and the Americans could decode all their most private communications for years to come. Does that make us clever or them stupid . . . or both?

No More Fibs

The lie detector—or, to give it its proper name, polygraph—has long been part of the paraphernalia used in the murky world of espionage. It's a tricky little gizmo involving four long, thin pens wired up to electronic sensors measuring pulse, breathing, and even sweating. One belt goes around the victim's waist, one around the wrist, and tiny electrodes are attached to the fingers to measure moisture (sweat to you). When switched on, the pens trace thin lines around a revolving disk of graph paper. The theory is that when someone tells a lie, the operator is supposed to be able to see erratic up-and-down movements on the paper. The British regarded the machine about as accurate as tossing a coin and really no more than an excitement detector. Not only that, but even if you could have detected a slight difference when someone was answering a delicate question (implying that they were fibbing), it was suspected by British Intelligence that the Soviets had a school that taught their agents methods of fooling the machine. This would become particularly useful if a spy wanted to pass on false information. As you will probably realize, the whole point of a lie detector would be missing.

By the Way

Despite changing its policy and dishing out lots of money on six brand-new, super-duper American lie detectors to test civil servants in crucial jobs, Britain threw them all away in 1985. Not only, I must add, because they didn't work but because the trade union wouldn't allow the bosses to use them on its members.

Satellites

No self-respecting spying nation should be without its own spy-in-the-sky Satellite Asset Management & Operations (SAMOs). The first ever was launched in California in 1961. It could, if it wanted, take photographs of a whole continent or of just your mom and dad lying on the beach. It can develop the pictures on board (without sending them out to be developed). It had a little satellite called a MIDAS, which, through its infrared detection kit, could tell if someone that it didn't like had launched a missile.

The Soviets, as we know, loved snooping and took to satellites like ducks to—er—espionage. They were said, in fact, to be far more interested in satellites for spying (with the eventual prize of domination of outer space) than putting a couple of guys on the boring old moon.

Nothing New under the Sun

Spying from the sky is not new, however. In the nineteenth century, European nations sent up hot air balloons to snoop on the enemy. During World War II, cameras were standard equipment on all fighter aircraft. These days everyone's up there. There are literally hundreds of satellites—Russian, Chinese, South African—all frantically taking pictures of each other and where they came from. The British are old hands at it. Despite the end of the Cold War, there's even a massive concrete bunker just north of London, where the navy keeps a constant watch on Russian ships, submarines, planes, or whatever.

Satellites linked to ships and extremely sensitive ground stations are now responsible for 85 percent of all surveillance. Huge computers work day and night to make sense of the jumble of signals they transmit. The British government's communication center employs a staggering 140,000 people and costs a large fortune to operate annually. Practically nothing escapes their notice.

By the Way

These days, cameras 200 miles above the earth can focus on stuff no larger than a foot long. The U.S. Big Bird satellites, probably the best in the world, can read a newspaper headline or tell whether a person's wearing glasses.

Did you know that in Russia the FSB (son of the KGB) is making all companies install a box (called STORM) so that everything they send through the Internet can be monitored?

Did you know that in the United States there have been various attempts by the government to stop ordinary people

using codes on the net? If the feds get their way, they will soon only allow certain codes to exist—those to which they already have a key or those that are easy to decode.

In other words—BIG BROTHER WILL SOON BE WATCHING US ALL!

The Soviets Play Our Games

There is strong evidence to believe that throughout the 1980s, up to 20,000 Soviet agents snuck into the West with the oddest instructions. They were to buy any kids' computer games they could find and take them back to Moscow to be examined. The poor old Russkies had fallen so far behind with their computer technology that even the simplest computer toys yielded relevant programming information. For all we know, the same chip used to steer an electric toy dump truck could have been adapted to guide a lethal missile (scary or what!). The joke is, through examining all these toys and games, they practically caught up with the West—and, much to the distress of the CIA, it cost them virtually nothing.

WHAT NEXT?

If you think about it, the whole intelligence business since the end of the Cold War should be withering. The fifty years of fist-shaking between the Soviet Union and the United States is over. Ninety percent of all espionage in the last fifty years was all about the Americans trying to find out secret-type things about the Soviets, and vice versa, while, of course, both were trying their best to stop the other doing the same. It was all like a huge, hopelessly expensive, unnecessarily complex game of chess with neither side revealing its moves.

You'd think that with the collapse of the Communist bloc that the need for the massive Soviet intelligence system would be greatly reduced. This was true to a point. But despite the massive cutbacks after the Cold War, in military and intelligence staffing, both Russia and the United States find it necessary to strengthen their intelligence services. It's a known fact that both sides are catching more spies than they ever did during World War II.

But all that's understood. More important are all the threats that seem almost more serious than anything the Russians or Americans could ever do to each other. Terrorism, drug trafficking, international financial crime, and industrial espionage are all alive and kicking and gaining strength wherever you look.

Whereas weapons always used to be difficult to get hold of, you or I, or even the archbishop of Canterbury, could go and buy just about anything from a pea shooter to a nuclear missile tomorrow through the Internet, providing we have enough in our piggy banks. We could even, if the money stretched far enough, have a private army fully ready in a matter of weeks—so watch it!

The cost of fighting the drug war in the United States topped $13 billion in 1994, and massive markets are opening up everywhere you look—especially in all of those ex-Communist countries that have had the door on fun nailed on so tight for so, so long.

As for terrorism—the rise of religious fanaticism that seems to be spreading its tentacles throughout the world is so scary I can hardly talk about it.

As for finding out what all these guys are up to, unlike the old days, it's all become more difficult. Terrorists don't just call each other up from their mom's phone anymore, and drug barons don't e-mail each other every five minutes, and no self-respecting arms dealers would go near a fax machine—oh no. They're all into the most sophisticated methods of communication (like pigeons), most times outwitting those who are trying to catch 'em.

REALLY BARRY! HOW LONG ARE YOU GOING TO BE ON THAT PHONE?

Who's Listening?

As we speak, an enormous battle is going on in cyberspace between all the intelligence services that are trying to control the Internet and all the civil liberty organizations that don't want them to. These days the way intelligence agencies work has been changing. All that tapping, bugging, mail rustling, and office-breaking-in is old news. The perfect spy works with ridiculously high-focused mikes, laser beams, and untraceable cell phones. Best (or worst) of all, use of this equipment often doesn't require a license.

But wait a minute, all this is in danger of going out of date, too. More and more communication goes via the Internet using e-mails and integrated service digital networks and it is notoriously unsafe. The trouble is, just as all the security services use the very latest in computer equipment, all the same stuff is available to you and me, too. Not only that, you can buy software to create some of the most sophisticated codes known to humankind—off the shelf. The cat is still stalking the mouse, but, day by day, the mouse is in danger of becoming bigger and cleverer than the cat.

End Piece

Before you all go and hide under the bed, let me assure you that the future isn't all doom and gloom—far from it. Believe it or not, it has suddenly dawned on our brilliant world leaders that the enemy of humankind might not actually be each other . . . but international crime. Instead of wasting all their not-very-hard-earned cash on trying to second-guess what their counterparts are up to, the great powers are beginning to pool their resources. Who knows, you might even get a situation where the heads of MI6, the KGB, and the CIA do lunch.

SPY SPEAK

Ag and Fish: stands for the British Ministry of Agriculture and Fisheries. What's it got to do with spies? In World War I, it was used as a cover address for intelligence staff. Throughout the 1950s, many resting spies had desk jobs at the ministry, and it was understood that when a spy was said to be at Ag and Fish it meant he had "gone to ground."

agent provocateur: an agent sent into another country to provoke (stir up) trouble

biographic leverage: good old-fashioned blackmail

black bag jobs: part of a agent's everyday work— everything from burglary to bribery to kidnapping to even murder

bleep box: a method of telephone tapping, by which codes and frequencies enable the operative to break into various telephone networks. Used by most intelligence services.

blown: the term used when an agent is found out

bugging: listening in when you shouldn't

burnt: an agent who has been discovered and whose services are—how shall I say?—no longer needed (so he's retired, fired, or killed)

cacklebladder: making an alive person look dead (chicken blood, etc.), which often helps in blackmailing and forcing a confession from enemy agents

cannon: the guy whose job it is to steal back the money given to an enemy agent for information. Not a career for the faint-hearted.

the Center: nickname for the KGB headquarters in Moscow

CIA: the U.S. Central Intelligence Agency, nicknamed "the Company." The CIA is involved in both intelligence and counterintelligence.

cobbler: the guy you go to for a forged passport

defector: someone who runs away from either their cause or their country

demote maximally: to kill someone

dirty tricks: term used for the darker antics of the CIA

disinformation: anything designed to discredit or fool your enemy: false documents, false messages, smear tactics—you name it

doctor: the police. Hence, when arrested, they say "he's gone to the doctor."

FBI: Federal Bureau of Investigation—part of the United States Department of Justice. Among other responsibilities, the FBI protects the United States from foreign espionage and terrorist activities.

field: the particular turf on which a particular spy works

the Firm: nickname for the British secret service

fix: CIA term meaning to blackmail or con

fluttered: to be quizzed by a lie detector

footwarmer: an amplifier used in radio transmission

fumigating: checking a building for bugs (electronic ones)

going private: leaving the secret service

harmonica bug: tiny microphone that goes in a telephone

hospital: prison—how appropriate!

illegal: a top-notch Russian spy sent with false passports to foreign countries

in the game: in the intelligence industry

KGB: Komitet Gosudarstvennoy Bezopasnosti (yay, abbreviations), meaning the Soviet Committee for State Security

legend: a fake life story used by a spy as cover

lion-tamer: the man used to "calm down" a sacked agent who starts making threats. Not usually a very nice guy.

magpie board: a small bunch of keys, wires, knives, small tools, even a miniature transmitter, carried by an agent to aid in escape if captured

measles: a murder done so well that it looks as if the deceased died of natural causes

MI5: Britain's counterintelligence bureau, called the Security Service

MI6: Britain's secret intelligence service, London-based but operating mainly abroad

mole: an agent sent to work with the enemy or rival company in order to spill their secrets

mozhno girl: a pretty girl recruited by the KGB to seduce Western targets and report back to base on their secrets

music box: radio transmitter

musician: radio transmitter's operator

naked: operating alone without any help from the outside

nash: from a Russian word meaning to belong to one's own side

orchestra: long-term agents who remain dormant until being asked, blackmailed, or bullied into service

pavement artists: surveillance teams

peep: the guy who takes secret photographs, especially in rotten conditions

piano study: radio operation

Piscine: meaning "swimming pool" in French, the nickname for the French secret service (because it's next to a swimming pool—duh)

plumbing: the undercover work necessary to stage a major operation

radar button: a gizmo that pinpoints its carrier's position anywhere in the world, used to get him or her out of trouble

raven: a handsome guy used to seduce women in the line of duty (rough job but someone's got to do it)

safe house: somewhere secret where an agent can seek sanctuary if things get hot

sanction: approval for a killing

scalp-hunter: an expert who detects genuine defectors from fakes. They also rat on anyone who looks like they're about to run for it.

setting-up: trapping someone. Typical scenario—a pretty girl lures the prey into a room packed with microphones and cameras.

shoe: a false passport

sister: a member of the lower ranks of female spies

sleeper: an agent working in deep cover for years in a foreign country

soap: well-known truth drug

son et lumière: information on camera and microphone obtained in a setup (French, meaning "sound and light")

spoofing: snooping on secret establishments from the air, term circa World War II. Special high-flying planes with the latest in long-distance digital cameras are used.

spook: an agent or intelligence gatherer

sweetener: money or gifts used to persuade a "target"

thermal detector: a gadget that can tell where someone has been lying or sitting (measuring butt heat, presumably)

thirty-three: an emergency

turned agent: someone who changes sides

walk-in: someone who offers services or information without being asked

wet affair: an operation that uses a professional killer to eliminate a spy whose services are no longer needed

What's your twenty?: Where the heck are you?

XX Committee: double cross committee set up to control double or turned agents in World War II

zoo: police station

FURTHER READING

Cormier, Robert. *I Am the Cheese*. New York: Random House, 1994.

Fleming, Fergus. *Tales of Real Spies*. Tulsa, OK: EDC Publications, 1998.

Josephson, Judith Pinkerton. *Allan Pinkerton: The Original Private Eye*. Minneapolis: Lerner Publications Company, 1996.

Lyons, Mary E. *Dear Ellen Bee: A Civil War Scrapbook of Two Union Spies*. New York: Atheneum, 2000.

Mello, Tara Baukus. *The Central Intelligence Agency*. New York: Chelsea House Publications, 2000.

Melton, Keith H., William Colby, and Oleg Kalugin. *The Ultimate Spy Book*. New York: DK Publishing, 1996.

Rogers, James T. *The Secret War: Espionage in WWII*. New York: Facts on File, 1991.

Thomas, Paul. *Undercover Agents (Rebels With a Cause)*. Milwaukee, WI: Raintree/Steck Vaughn, 1998.

Wiese, Jim. *Spy Science: 40 Secret-Sleuthing, Code-Cracking, Spy-Catching, Activities for Kids*. New York: John Wiley & Sons, 1996.

Yancey, Diane. *Spies*. San Diego, CA: Lucent Books, 2001.

Yost, Graham. *Spies in the Sky*. New York: Facts On File, 1990.

WEBSITES

General Information

Cold War Espionage
<http://www.cnn.com/SPECIALS/cold.war/experience/spies/>

International Spy Museum
<http://www.spymuseum.org>

MI5, The Security Service
<http://www.mi5.gov.uk/>

Secrets, Lies, and Atomic Spies
<http://www.pbs.org/wgbh/nova/venona/>

Spy Fact of the Day
<http://www.randomhouse.com/features/spybook/archive.html>

Spy Letters of the American Revolution
<http://www.si.umich.edu/spies/>

Interactive

CIA's Homepage for Kids
<http://www.cia.gov/cia/ciakids/index.html>

FBI Youth
<http://www.fbi.gov/kids/6th12th/6th12th.htm>

The Spywatch Adventure
<http://www.bbc.co.uk/education/lookandread/intro.htm>

INDEX

ABOUT THE AUTHOR

John Farman has worked as a commercial illustrator and a cartoonist and has written more than thirty nonfiction books for children. He lives in London, England.